Fairy

the Art of
Jasmine Becket-Griffith

Fairy

the Art of
Jasmine Becket-Griffith

written & illustrated by Jasmine Becket-Griffith

edited by Kachina Glenn & Grant Singleton

www.strangeling.com

Published in 2005 by Jasmine Becket-Griffith

www.strangeling.com

Jasmine Becket-Griffith
PO BOX 470932
Celebration, FL 34747-0932

Copyright © 2005 by Jasmine Becket-Griffith. 27269-BECK
Library of Congress number: 2005905998
ISBN: Softcover   0-9789667-5-9

Distributed by *LTT/The Fairy Society*
Ontario, California USA
www.lazytimetoys.com
www.thefairysociety.com

Contents

Hazel Fairy
A beautiful hazel toned fairy painted in my trademark style.
16"x20" acrylic paints on canvas.

Introduction

The mundane world can be a very, very dull place.

It is my goal as an "artist" to try to alleviate the boredom. I want to bring a little magic into the world, the only way I know how - with my paintings. When I first decided to pursue art as a career and as a hobby, I knew from the start that I would be a fantasy artist. I enjoy creating my own little worlds with my own characters and stories. And I enjoy sharing them with others even more!

It was this that led me to create this book. After years of questions from fans- "When are you going to do a book?" "When are you going to do your *own* book?" "Why don't you have a book?"- I knew it was just a matter of time.

So here you go - this book is for you. I've selected some of my most popular paintings, along with some of my personal favourites. This book focuses on my fairy artwork, so prepare yourself for "things with wings"! The spirit of Faery is growing stronger in this world, and by spreading the word through art and story, it will hopefully continue to do so!

There are all kinds of faeries in this book - from beautiful traditional faeries with flowers and sparkles to the gothic fae of the night with sinister gleams in their eyes. All of them are portrayed here in my original acrylic paintings. There is a little bit of something for everyone here, and whether you have been following my artwork for years or if this is your very first introduction to it, I genuinely hope that you enjoy this book.

Until next time,

Jasmine Becket-Griffith
(aka Strangeling)

Bed of Frogs
I love frogs and toads, and this painting shows it! Some people who are
more squeamish about them have told me this is a nightmarish scene, but I find it cozy.
A 12"x16" acrylic painting on canvas.

Faeries and Animals

Faeries share a special bond with the animal world. Animals have keen senses and seem to lack the prejudice most humans have when approaching the unknown. Because of this, they can often see and even interact with faeries while their human companions would never suspect such a thing! Since faeries typically live on the outskirts of civilized areas they regularly encounter wild animals and sometimes even form close friendships with them.

I explore the relationships between faeries and animals in a lot of my paintings and I consider it to be a constant source of inspiration.

The Handsome Frog

I've always thought that frogs have a very goblin-like quality to them. It would only make sense that they would be friends with faeries! I frequently paint faeries alongside frogs, and this piece was an excuse to paint a frog in his finery. A 24"x18" acrylic painting on canvas.

9

To Love a Frog
I do paint a lot of frogs - I've always loved them, and living in Florida they are a part of daily life. This is a sweet painting, of a fairy girl who loves her frog.   She actually prefers frogs over people, and sometimes I can't say that I blame her....
This is an acrylic painting on canvas measuring 12"x16".

A Ferret and His Fairy
I've always thought of ferrets as being somewhat magical. Anybody who has owned a
ferret probably knows what I mean! They exist on the edge of reason and can surely
see the faeries! This is a 12"x16" acrylic painting on canvas.

Two of a Kind
Another painting featuring a ferret! They might always feel a little different among the rest of their friends, but together this pair of beauties are two of a kind. Artistically this was a fun piece to create - very little paint was actually used! It is an acrylic painting on a 12"x16" canvas.

A Prickly Situation
Hedgehogs are amazing creatures and seem to possess magical qualities themselves! I had a hedgehog for a pet and found that in addition to being dear little animals, they are indeed quite prickly. This is a 16"x12" acrylic painting on canvas.

Elf Maiden and Her Dragon
Faery folk have a close affinity with animals of all kinds: those known to the human
population as well as those long considered mythical! A 12"x16" acrylic painting on canvas.

Bumble Bee Fairy
A 16"x20" acrylic painting on canvas.

Green Dragonling
A custom painting for my friend Justine!
9"x12" acrylics on canvas.

A Millipede Friend
A 12"x16" acrylic painting on canvas.

Anise Swallowtail
This fairy has the wings of the Anise Swallowtail
butterfly and is cradling a caterpillar of the same
species. 12"x16" acrylics on canvas.

Strangeling's Felines by Carrie Hawks
No, this isn't one of my paintings!
This is the painting that my friend
Carrie Hawks did of my two cats,
Azrael and Quan-Yin, as part of our
"Pet Portrait Swap" for an art show.
It is 12"x9" acrylics on canvas.
My painting of *her* cats can be seen
below. To see more of Carrie's art,
check out her website at
www.tigerpixie.com

"Pixie Cats"
This was my side of the "Pet Portrait Swap" - a painting of Carrie Hawks' two
kitties, Zoe and Tabby. I'm very surprised that they didn't try to bat at the faeries
while I was painting them! This one is 16"x12" - acrylics on canvas.

Allura
A particularly *alluring* fairy of the night, with large luminous eyes for night vision,
lush green leaves wet with dew, and starlight in her wings.
One of my largest paintings, 24"x30" acrylic on canvas.

Night Faeries

Some of the most beautiful and certainly the most mysterious faeries are those of the Nocturnal variety. These are the least likely to be seen by human eyes, for they blend into the shadows and avoid bright places. You may occasionally feel the soft brush of a wing against your hand or your cheek, but that is the extent of most people's experience with Night Faeries.

As an artist who often embraces a darker aesthetic, I've found that these faeries of the night regularly find their way into my paintings. Whether they are revelling in the starlight or communing silently with the celestial bodies of the cosmos, I try my best to capture that moment in paint, hopefully before the sun rises.

By Starlight
Kind of a self portrait, like a lot of my work. This golden haired fairy is sharing
a moment with her butterfly friend under the stars.
An acrylic painting on a 16"x12" canvas.

Starry Night Fairy

One of my most popular paintings, one of my largest, and certainly one of my best! This
fairy brings a bit of magic to an old crumbling portal. The blue and orange colours provide
a superb contrast. This one is a 24"x30" acrylic painting on canvas.

Pink Butterfly Fairy
A custom painting for my friend
Heidi. 9"x12" acrylics on canvas.

Just a Little Fairy
A quiet fairy sitting thoughtfully in the night.
A 12"x16" acrylic painting on canvas.

Prismatic Fairy
A rainbow toned fairy contemplating life up in the cosmos.
A 20"x16" acrylic painting on canvas.

The Star Child

Another fairy of the Night. Somewhere up in the sky, or maybe out in the cosmos - the
Star Child, shimmering with the light of the stars. The placement of highlights was very
integral to the "shimmery" feel of this painting. It is 16"x20" - acrylics on canvas.

Halloween Night
A festive fairy on Halloween Night!
A 12"x16" acrylic painting on canvas.

Just About Midnight
A fairy "moon-bathing" on a mushroom.
12"x16" acrylic painting on canvas.

Fairy of the Changing Moons
A wide-eyed fairy communing with
the changing moon phases.
18"x24" acrylics on canvas.

Fairy by Moonlight
A fun experiment in painting all
in shades of blue!
12"x16" acrylics on canvas

Looking for Faeries
A slightly different style for me, somewhat inspired by both the Pre-Raphaelite and the
Impressionist movements. This maiden (modeled after my friend Michaela) is lost and
doesn't seem to see the faeries below. It is an 18"x24" acrylic painting on canvas.

Faeries in Nature

Most faeries live out in natural areas, away from the congestion and pollution of urban life. There they are left to themselves, blending into the foliage and enjoying the outdoors. Faeries are comfortable in nature and adapt to a variety of climates: tropical warmth, temperate forests, boggy swamps, even the frozen tundra.

Nature is one of my biggest inspirations. While I enjoy painting faeries in a variety of plants and environments, you will no doubt notice that most of my paintings are inspired by the local swamps and wetlands here in Florida.

Swamp Spirit
Many faeries are difficult to see in their native environments. Not only has this young fairy begun to take on the colouration of the swamp, she has also constructed her garments from the local plant life!
An 18"x14" acrylic painting on canvas.

Green Butterfly Fantasy
Faeries in the wilds of Nature are often difficult to see. One possible reason for this is that
they are usually very well camouflaged. The fairy in this painting is a good example. With her
green skin and mottled green leaves, few people would take a second glance. She is also a
good example of the "mimicry" found often in the fairy world. Many fairy wings closely
resemble butterfly wings, and most people rarely take the time to double-check butterflies
as they flutter by. This painting is 16"x12" - acrylics on canvas.

Hiding in the Vines
A fairy emerging from some slimey vines!
A 12"x16" acrylic painting on canvas.

Swamp Beauty
Swamp faeries are often green, making them
difficult to see. 8"x10" acrylic painting on canvas.

Poison Ivy Fairy
A protector of the rather annoying plant.
8"x10" acrylic painting on canvas.

A Bashful Fairy
Shy faeries are even more difficult to find....
14"x18" acrylic painting on canvas.

Keeper of the Green Orbs

When I'm in need of a little inspiration I often take walks in the woods and swamps around
my home. This painting is based on a real hollow tree near my house that seemed magical....
A 12"x16" acrylic painting on canvas.

Sparkling Among the Flowers

Nothing goes better with faeries than flowers!
Faeries can often be found near flowers; they are
attracted by the sweet smells and the bright
colours. When looking for faeries, examining
flowers closely is a good idea - be sure to keep
an eye out for shimmering dust or twinkling
sparkles! Many a fairy has had her cover blown by
too much pixie dust! This was a fun little piece
to paint; I always enjoy working with a bright
colour combination. It is an 8"x10" acrylic
painting on canvas.

Swamp Fairy

A beautiful fairy bathing in the swamp, picking bog lilies!
This painting is inspired by a swamp near my house. It's one of my favourite pieces and
is also one of my largest - a 30"x24" acrylic painting on canvas.

Queen Mab

Here is Queen Mab of the faeries - of Shakespearian fame and Arthurian legend. I had a
wonderful time painting this. If you look closely you will see many of the Queen's faery
subjects peering back out at you! It is an 18"x24" acrylic painting on canvas.

Forest Fae
A fairy child in a misty forest. This painting was inspired by a foggy part of Golden Gate Park in San Francisco. It is a peaceful painting - the fairy seems to be at harmony with the natural beauty surrounding her. It is a 14"x18" acrylic painting on canvas.

Tribal Fairy
A magical fairy living deep in an ancient forest. She has blue woad tattoos on her body and a magical spear to protect herself. This cute little character first appeared in my Queen Mab painting! A 16"x12" acrylic painting on canvas.

Hamadryad

A hamadryad is a sort of wood nymph typically associated with one specific tree that she dedicates her life to protecting. This beauty is so encompassed within her tree that it is difficult to tell where she begins and the tree ends! This is an 18"x24" acrylic painting on canvas.

Wood Nymph

A spritely green wood nymph in the deep forest on a moonlit night. There are strange creatures
in these woods! So many pairs of eyes are staring at her, yet her glance is cast downward. It's
one of my earlier paintings and it is very special to me.
It's a 16"x20" acrylic painting on canvas.

Lamenting the Forgotten

This is a rather dark and melancholy painting. Modeled by my lovely friend Ophelia, this vampiric fae creature is lamenting a long forgotten grave. The red accents in this piece really stand out against the gloomy background. A 16"x20" acrylic painting on canvas.

Dark Faeries

Not every fairy is all smiles and sunshine! Many, many faeries walk a far darker path. The world of Faery is quite varied, and there are a lot of bad seeds full of mischief and malice. Whether they are just angst-ridden young fae with bad attitudes or blood-thirsty mistresses of black magic, the Dark Faeries are a whole realm unto themselves.

The Dark Faeries are irresistable to me as an artist. Here there are no limits of convention and good grace. Their tricks may go beyond hiding buttons or sprinkling pixie dust, but they are no less beautiful, and perhaps even more alluring in their wickedness.

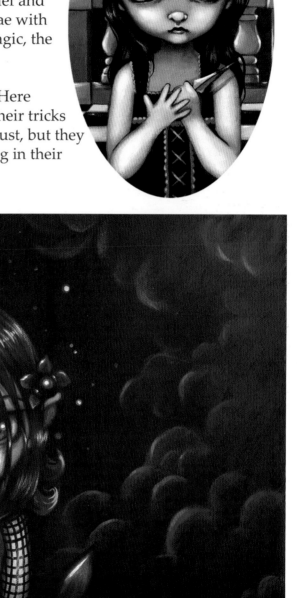

Belladonna's Gift
At first this might seem to be just a lovely young fairy offering a gift of a sweet berry. However, upon closer inspection, the berry is from none other than the poisonous belladonna plant (aka Deadly Nightshade)! A 16"x12" acrylic painting on canvas.

Biomechanical Fairy
A very strange painting indeed - a bizarre faery creature being pieced together
in a mysterious factory. It is a mostly monochromatic piece with just a hint of murky blue.
I sometimes enjoy painting with a very limited palette - it forces me to focus on gradation
of tone, form and shading. This painting is kind of a nod to HR Giger, one of my
inspirations and the undisputed master of "biomechanical" art.
This is an acrylic painting on canvas measuring 12"x16".

Arcane Ritual Fairy #4
The fourth installment in my series based on
old alchemical texts. 12"x16" acrylics on canvas.

Fairy Oracle?
She thinks she has a powerful dark relic, but
it looks like a plastic Magic 8-Ball to me!
12"x16" acrylic painting on canvas.

A Smirking Fairy
I'm not sure what she's smirking about, but it
can't be good.... A 12"x16" acrylic painting on canvas.

Gothling #8
The eighth installment in my popular
"Gothlings" series featuring grumpy goth
faeries. 9"x12" acrylics on canvas.

Hunger Pains
An undead self-portrait.
16"x20" acrylic painting on canvas.

Gothling #1
The first in my popular "Gothlings" series.
Acrylic on canvas, 9"x12".

Red Winged Fairy
This was really fun to do - it's all monochromatic outside of the blood-red
details which really make this piece come to life! 16"x12" acrylic paints on canvas.

Horned Fairy
This little cutie has a tricksy gleam in her eye!
An experiment in bold contrasting forms, this was a fun piece to paint.
It is an acrylic painting on canvas measuring 11"x14".

Gothling #7
The seventh installment in my "Gothlings"
series. 9"x12" acrylic painting on canvas.

Delphine
A portrait I painted of my friend and fellow fantasy
artist Delphine Lévesque Demers (www.zerick.com).
Acrylic painting on 12"x16" canvas.

Ice Fairy
A portrait of my friend Celeste,
a professional model
12"x16" acrylic on canvas.

Pumpkin Pixie
A Halloween fairy with her pet pumpkin.
Acrylic painting on a 12"x16" canvas.

Voodoo in the Bayou
Swamps and bayous are rife with all kinds of faery mischief! This sinister beauty
is clearly up to no good. This painting is 12"x16" - acrylics on canvas.

Fairy Queen Titania

Here is the beautiful Titania - Queen of the Fairy Court. Best known from Shakespeare's
"A Midsummer Night's Dream", I've always found her to be a fascinating character in the
world of faery. This is one of several paintings I've done of her - 16"x20" acrylics on canvas.

Faeries with Friends and Family

While many faeries do live a solitary life, others prefer to live in family groups or in other community settings. Faeries can be very social creatures!

The world of Faery encompasses a wide variety of "species" of faeries, yet they all share common bonds and often spend time with each other. It is fun as an artist to figure out how to show the faeries with their relatives, children, neighbors, or even their adversaries.

Faery Folk Alliance
I did this painting to show how varied the world of Faery really is! Not all fae are pretty girls with wings. This was an incredibly fun painting to do - so much colour and detail!
This is a 20"x16" acrylic painting on canvas.

Fairy Christmas

I painted this right around Christmas time, and it is full of Christmassy goodness!
I like to think that faeries hold a lot of holidays, feasts, and celebrations, and I had a fun
time deciding how their house would be decorated for the season. These three sisters
(not unlike myself and my two sisters) are having a cozy night at home on Christmas Eve.
There are a lot of fun little details in this piece - their Christmas tree is a twig potted in
a broken human-sized Christmas ornament, and there are all kinds of Christmas goodies
on their table. Artistically, this was a study in lighting as there are two light sources in
this scene: the cold moonlight on the right, and the warm fireplace on the left.
This is a 20"x16" acrylic painting on canvas.

Fairy Dwelling #1: UnderHill

This is the first installment in my "Fairy Dwelling" series. This series was suggested to me by my father while we were walking on a nature trail down in the Florida Keys. He thought that it would be neat if I showed the homes that the faeries made for themselves! These faeries obviously live on the edge of an area also inhabited by humans. If you look closely at their home, you will see a lot of it is made out of bits of rubbish and litter - all kinds of human detritus. You may even recognize some of the labels on the beverages in there. This was a fun painting to do - I truly enjoyed throwing in all of the little details, and I also liked working with a very specific light source (their cozy window!). This painting is 20"x16" and is acrylic on canvas.

Dark Haired Beauties
Two raven-haired faeries painted with varying degrees of
stylization. A bit of a self-portrait in both of them!
16"x12" acrylics on canvas.

Lustrous Faeries
I'm not sure if these are her children or just diminutive friends,
but they sure have pretty hair! A fun painting to do, both in style and
in colour. 16"x12" acrylic painting on canvas.

Lady of the Faeries
A majestic faery lady with her three
little children. 11"x14" acrylic painting
on canvas.

Fairy Cluster
This painting was a fun excuse to paint a variety
of types of faeries. There's one based
on me and another based on my friend Christine.
A 16"x20" acrylic painting on canvas.

Hiding in the Swamp
I think this is a fairy with her two younger sisters.
A 16"x12" acrylic painting on canvas.

Green Goddess
A regal fairy goddess with many of her fairy friends - all painted in shades of green!
Green is my favourite colour and, as you may have noticed by now, it often dominates
my paintings. This is a 16"x20" acrylic painting on canvas.

The Butterfly Faeries
Three fairy sisters!
A 16"x20" acrylic painting on canvas.

Protectors of the Vines
A very strange family of faeries.
A different palette than my usual work,
this is almost completely monochromatic.
12"x16" acrylic paints on canvas.

Below Zero
She loves him, but he can't leave his cold climate-
hot cocoa. The things you put up with for love!

so she buys warm clothes and drinks
A 16"x12" acrylic painting on canvas.

Fairy in My Window
A cute little fairy who has just flitted up for a brief stop at a crumbling stone window!
One of my trademark "wide eyed" faeries, this painting always makes me smile.
This is a 12"x16" acrylic painting on canvas.

Other Faeries

Since the world of Faery is so large and varied, there are quite a few faeries that simply cannot be classified into any one group or another. The need to categorize everything is a very *human* idiosyncrasy, and the faeries just won't always cooperate.

Because of this, many of my fairy paintings cannot be easily classified. In this chapter you will find a wide selection of strange and beautiful faeries of all kinds that didn't quite fit anywhere else.

Labyrinth Fairy
Faery trickery goes hand in hand with mazes and labyrinths. This is actually a "working" maze that I designed myself! A 16"x12" acrylic painting on canvas.

Thoughtful Fairy #3
An older painting of mine - acrylics
and watercolours on paper, 8"x10".

Blue Ribbon Fairy
An acrylic painting on canvas,
18"x24".

Making a Wish
This is a special painting I did for
my friend Laura Wojtowicz!
A 9"x12" acrylic painting on canvas.

Nude Fairy Drake
A mostly monochromatic painting
of a more realistically rendered figure
juxtaposed with a flat stylized background.
A 12"x16" acrylic painting on canvas.

Spearmint Sprite
One of the two "mint faeries" that I've
painted - her sister is Peppermint Pretty.
9"x12" acrylic paints on canvas.

Peppermint Pretty
Spearmint Sprite's sister.
She's the good sister, pretty in pink!
9"x12" acrylic paints on canvas.

Fairy with a Sweet Tooth
Some faeries have a definite attraction
to sweets. This was a fun painting with
all of the candy and colours!
9"x12" acrylic paints on canvas.

Licorice Fairy
Black and red is one of my favourite
colour combinations. This cutie loves
licorice of any kind!
9"x12" acrylic paints on canvas.

Captive Fairy
A naughty little fairy tied up with ribbons! I really like the bright magenta and green colour combination. This is a 12"x16" acrylic painting on canvas.

Autumn Enchantress
A more realistically painted portrait
of my friend Tina!
A 12"x16" acrylic painting on canvas.

Lost... but Not Worried
She's lost her way, but she's not too
concerned about it.
Acrylic paints on a 12"x16" canvas.

The Last Leaves
A nearly monochromatic painting with
just a few hints of green.
9"x12" acrylic paints on canvas.

A Flutter of Wings
A moment of reflection amongst the
hurried bustle of fairy wings.
16"x20" acrylic paints on canvas.

53

White Witch of the Storm
From Hungarian fairy tales, this is Szepasszony - the White Witch of the Storm. She
is the bringer of storms and she revels in dancing in the rain and hail. Her dances create
"fairy circles" in the grass, and it is considered unwise for mortals to enter these circles.
A large painting - 24"x30" acrylic on canvas.

Sienna
A lovely dark eyed fairy. I named her
after the paint I used for her hair -
Burnt Sienna. 12"x16" acrylics on canvas.

Purple Ribbon Fairy
A slightly worried fairy tied up with
pretty purple ribbons!
12"x16" acrylic paints on canvas.

Harvest Fairy
A still life with a faery twist!
16"x12" acrylic paints on canvas.

Sisters
An earlier piece of mine, I made this painting
for my mother. It's based on myself and
my two sisters. 9"x12" acrylic on canvas.

Pensive Fairy
A very small painting - a quick study
of a fairy deep in thought.
5"x7" acrylic paints on canvas.

Titania and Bottom
A scene from Shakespeare's "A Midsummer Night's Dream".   In this painting I have
shown Titania with her donkey-headed paramour Bottom - the two are sharing a quiet
moment. This is an early painting of mine, actually done for a school assignment.
A 20"x16" acrylic painting on canvas.

La Finestra Verde
La Finestra Verde is Italian for "The Green Window". This is a dramatically lighted
piece, with this melancholy dear emerging from the darkness. 12"x16" acrylic on canvas.

Painting Tutorial #1: Eyes

For those of you interested in the more technical side of artwork, I thought I would prepare a couple of short tutorials showing my painting techniques!

As I mentioned before, I often use myself as a model in my paintings. Hey - I'm always available, and I don't charge myself sitting fees! Sometimes I use a mirror, or sometimes I'll make my husband take photos of me for reference. For this tutorial I will use a photograph of my own eyes, as pictured to your left.

Every painting starts off as a blank piece of paper, or in this case, canvas. This is a scrap of flat canvas I cut to 5"x3". Since I hate blank canvases, and I don't want any white grains showing through, I typically paint it all black before doing anything else.

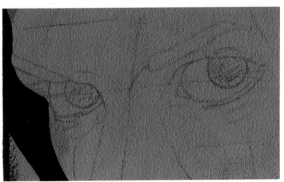

In this next step, I blocked in the general face shape using a base colour. For the base colour I try to choose what will be the darkest shadow colour in the face. I then make a layout sketch using a graphite pencil. The sketch is very important - I keep working the sketch until it looks just right. In this piece, the most important lines are the angles of the eyes and nose. I usually draw complete circles for the irises of the eyes and will erase the excess later. It's okay to have a messy sketch - it will all be covered with paint very soon of course!

I then take some thinned black paint (I use liquid or "fluid" acrylic paints, and use water to thin it if needed) and I go over the parts of the sketch that I am happy with and want to keep in the painting. This is just for my own layout purposes - again, this will all be covered up with paint very soon! I use a small "script liner" sized brush for this part. I have found that synthetic brushes work best with my technique, and of course being a vegetarian I always prefer to use man-made fibers. I like the "golden taklon" bristles the best!

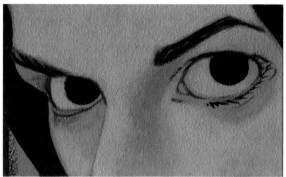

Here is where the actual "painting" begins! With the basic lines and shapes already in place, I am now focusing on colour and shading. I enjoy blending my own skin tones rather than using them "straight out of the bottle". I paint in many very thin layers of paint, often using a hairdryer to speed the dry time between layers. At this stage I am using shadow colours of purple and blue with a creamy opaque base for the bulk of the skin tone.

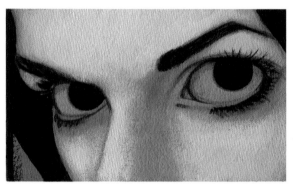

Many layers later, I am still building up with more thin layers of paint. I use somewhat of a "glazing" technique - basically I continually add layers of lighter and more transparent colours on top of darker and more opaque colours. I use a small round brush for this part of the painting, taking time to define the edges with a small script liner brush from time to time. For a softer look I very often use my fingers to smudge!

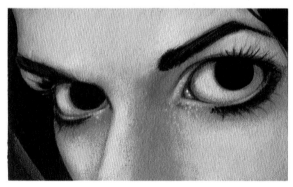

I am still glazing away with more and more layers at this point! Since the fluid acrylic paints I use are so very thin, and I often thin them further with water, the surface of the painting is still very flat despite the many layers. I like a smooth surface on my paintings, with very little *impasto*. Also at this point I have started to add details like makeup, the eyelashes, etc. I've also added several layers on the "whites" of the eyes, which aren't actually white at all - rather more pinkish and creamy blue.

Here I am finished! The last steps I took were adding the highlights. I think that with my technique, the highlights are the most important step. They can really "make" or "break" the painting, especially when painting eyes. When adding the final layers of highlights, I use a pure white paint that has been heavily thinned with water on a small soft brush. The first layers of highlights are mostly water, and I then increase the opacity with more paint for the final touch. It is important to put a lot of focus on the eyes of your subjects - they can truly captivate the viewers!

Painting Tutorial #2: A Faery Frog

Though this tutorial specifically shows how I painted a winged fantasy frog, the techniques outlined here can be applied to nearly any kind of painting, froggy or not!

I've cut another scrap of canvas into a 5"x3" rectangle. Again, I start by painting the canvas black. I'm planning on having a solid black background for this piece, so it's important that I paint a good opaque black base coat onto the canvas. I always buy rolls of canvas that have been pre-gessoed for acrylic paints, so I don't need to pre-treat the surface before I begin.

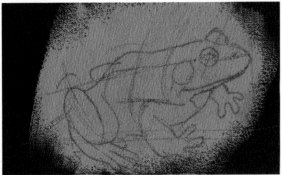

Since this is going to be a greenish frog and it will be centrally located in the painting, I've smudged in a green base coat in the middle of the canvas on which I can begin my sketch. I've drawn and painted many, many frogs, so there was no need for any kind of photo reference. I use a regular graphite pencil to sketch with - it's a little sloppy and smudgy at first, and I've made a few mistakes, but it doesn't matter since in the end it will all be covered up with paint!

I've refined the layout sketch a little more and have covered up the parts of the sketch I won't be using. I used an opaque black paint with my small script liner brush to come right up to the edges of what will be the frog's body and in between his froggy toes. Since this is such a tiny painting, I mostly will be using the script liner sized brush.

At this point I have gone over my primary sketch lines with a thinned black paint. Now I am beginning to put down the colours. This is the very first layer after the sketch is complete - a dark transparent green pigment, providing a good base tone. This will be the first of several dozen layers!

At this stage, I have filled in a couple of base layers on the frog's skin. I've used a few different shades of green to give it depth. I have also sketched in some wings with a white Derwent watercolour pencil. If I am laying out a sketch on a dark background, I often use a white watercolour pencil - that way the sketch will show up clearly and will also wipe away with water.

I have now added still more layers of paint on the frog's skin, including a darker cream colour for his underbelly. I have also started to fill in the outlines of the wings I sketched earlier. I want the pattern and colour of the wings to resemble those of a Monarch butterfly. I have selected a dark brownish-orange for the base colour of the wings since that is the darkest shade that will appear on the finished wings.

Here I have continued adding multiple layers of thinned paint on the wings and on the frog himself. At this stage I am no longer adding paint on the parts of the frog that would be more shaded (such as under the arms, below the legs, etc.), so there is more of a three dimensional effect.

Now it is finished! My final steps were to detail the wings with black veins and white spots (all done with my tiny script liner brush) to build up the yellow highlights on the wings, and to build up the yellow and then white layers of highlight on the frog's body and face. As always, I put a lot of thought into where I add the highlights to give the picture a sense of depth and substance.

Jasmine Becket-Griffith
This is me. I may look a bit familiar since I often use myself as a model
for my paintings. Even my "wide eyed" stylized faeries are actually little
caricatures of myself.

From Jasmine

Thank you so much for taking the time to read my book. I hope that you enjoyed it!

I've dedicated my life to my artwork. It has encompassed everything I do. When I wake up each morning I begin painting, and when I am not painting I'm thinking about what I will be painting next. I am lucky in that my obsession happens to be something so very productive and that it provides enjoyment for others as well.

I live here in Celebration, Florida with my husband (and full-time assistant) Matt and our two cats, Azrael and Quan-Yin. I'm 25 years old and I spend my days creating art.

Being the nerd that I am, my primary platform for showcasing my art is on the internet. If you've enjoyed this book, *please* take the time to get online and check out the rest of my stuff!

My website, store, and online gallery:
www.strangeling.com

My eBay store where you can buy my prints, merchandise and original paintings:
stores.ebay.com/StrangelingsArtGallery

or just "search by seller" up on eBay by my user ID:
strangeling

My online journal where I update every day with my new artwork, daily thoughts, photos, stuff about my personal life, etc.:
jasminetoad.livejournal.com

For questions or comments:
JasmineToad@aol.com

Acknowledgments

There are a lot of people to whom I owe a great deal of thanks.

I'd like to thank my family, especially my sisters, for their love and friendship.

I would like to thank my fans who have supported me over these
many years. Without you guys, there would be no book.

I would like to thank the internet.

And finally I would like to thank my Matty for putting up with me.